CONNECT BIBLE STUDIES

Chocolat

Joanne Harris
(Black Swan, 1999)

Temptation
Community
Friendship
Change

CONNECT BIBLE STUDIES: Chocolat

Published in this format by Scripture Union, 207-209 Queensway, Bletchley, MK2 2EB, England.

Scripture Union is an international Christian charity working with churches in more than 130 countries providing resources to bring the good news about Jesus Christ to children, young people and families — and to encourage them to develop spiritually through the Bible and prayer.

As well as a network of volunteers, staff and associates who run holidays, church-based events and school Christian groups, Scripture Union produces a wide range of publications and supports those who use the resources through training programmes.

Email: info@scriptureunion.org.uk
Internet: www.scriptureunion.org.uk

© Damaris Trust, PO Box 200, Southampton, SO17 2DL.

Damaris Trust enables people to relate Christian faith and contemporary culture. It helps them to think about the issues within society from a Christian perspective and to explore God's truth as it is revealed in the Bible. Damaris provides resources via the Internet, workshops, publications and products.

Email: office@damaris.org
Internet: www.damaris.org

All rights reserved. Generally, any part of this publication may only be reproduced or transmitted in any form or by any means with prior permission of the copyright holder. But purchasers of this set of Connect Bible Studies may print, photocopy or otherwise reproduce the Members' Sheets for use in any group in which they are actively involved. In addition, the complete set may be printed or photocopied once for use in a single group.

ALSO AVAILABLE AS AN ELECTRONIC DOWNLOAD: www.connectbiblestudies.com

Chief editor: Nick Pollard
Consultant Editor: Andrew Clark
Managing Editor: Di Archer
Written by Di Archer, Caroline Puntis, Tony Watkins

First published 2001
ISBN 1 85999 608 6

British Library Cataloguing-in-Publication Data: a catalogue record for this book is available from the British Library.

Cover design and print production by:
CPO, Garcia Estate, Canterbury Road, Worthing, West Sussex BN13 1BW.

Other titles in this series:

Harry Potter and the Goblet of Fire ISBN 1 85999 578 0
The Matrix ISBN 1 85999 579 9
U2: All that you can't leave behind ISBN 1 85999 580 2
Billy Elliot ISBN 1 85999 581 0
TV Game Shows ISBN 1 85999 609 4
How to be Good ISBN 1 85999 610 8
Destiny's Child: Survivor ISBN 1 85999 613 2

And more titles following — check www.connectbiblestudies.com for latest titles or ask at any good Christian bookshop.

Using Connect Bible Studies

What Are These Studies?

These innovative home group Bible studies have two aims. Firstly, we design them to enable group members to dig into their Bibles and get to know them better. Secondly, we aim to help members to think through topical issues in a Biblical way. Hence the studies are based on a current popular book or film etc. The issues raised by these are the subjects for the Bible studies.

We do not envisage that all members will always be able to watch the films or read the books, or indeed that they will always want to. A summary is always provided. However, our vision is that knowing about these films and books empowers Christians to engage with friends and colleagues about them. Addressing issues from a Biblical perspective gives Christians confidence that they know what they think, and can bring a distinctive angle to bear in conversations.

The studies are produced in sets of four — i.e. four weeks' worth of group Bible Study material. These are available in print published by Scripture Union from your local Christian bookshop, or via the Internet at www.connectbiblestudies.com. Anyone can sign up for a free monthly email newsletter that announces the new studies and provides other information (sign up on the Connect Bible Studies website at www.connectbiblestudies.com/uk/register).

How Do I Use Them?

We design the studies to stimulate creative thought and discussion within a Biblical context. Each section therefore has a range of questions or options from which you as leader may choose in order to tailor the study to your group's needs and desires. Different approaches may appeal at different times, so the studies aim to supply lots of choice. Whilst adhering to the main aim of corporate Bible study, some types of questions may enable this for your group better than others — so take your pick.

Group members should be supplied with the appropriate sheet that they can fill in, each one also showing the relevant summary.

Leader's notes contain:

1. Opening Questions

These help your group settle in to discussion, whilst introducing the topics. They may be straightforward, personal or creative, but are aiming to provoke a response.

2. Summary

We suggest the summary of the book or film will follow now, read aloud if necessary. There may well be reactions that group members want to express even before getting on to the week's issue.

3. Key Issue

Again, either read from the leader's notes, or summarised.

4. Bible Study

Lots of choice here. Choose as appropriate to suit your group — get digging into the Bible. Background reading and texts for further help and study are suggested, but please use the material provided to inspire your group to explore their Bibles as much as possible. A concordance might be a handy standby for looking things up. A commentary could be useful too, such as the New Bible Commentary 21st century edition (IVP, 1994). The idea is to help people to engage with the truth of God's word, wrestling with it if necessary but making it their own.

Don't plan to work through every question here. Within each section the two questions explore roughly the same ground but from different angles or in different ways. Our advice is to take one question from each section. The questions are open-ended so each ought to yield good discussion — though of course any discussion in a Bible study may need prompting to go a little further.

5. Implications

Here the aim is to tie together the perspectives gained through Bible study and the impact of the book or film. The implications may be personal, a change in worldview, or new ideas for relating to non-churchgoers. Choose questions that adapt to the flow of the discussion.

6. Prayer

Leave time for it! We suggest a time of open prayer, or praying in pairs if the group would prefer. Encourage your members to focus on issues from your study that had a particular impact on them. Try different approaches to prayer — light a candle, say a prayer each, write prayers down, play quiet worship music — aim to facilitate everyone to relate to God.

7. Background Reading

You will find links to some background reading on the Connect Bible Studies website: www.connectbiblestudies.com/

8. Online Discussion

You can discuss the studies online with others on the Connect Bible Studies website at www.connectbiblestudies.com/discuss/

Scriptures referred to are taken from the Holy Bible, New International Version (NIV). Copyright (c) 1973, 1978, 1984 by International Bible Society. Other Bible translations can, of course, be used for the studies and having a range of translations in a group can be helpful and useful in discussion.

Chocolat
Joanne Harris (Black Swan, 1999)

Part One: Temptation

*This is why I came to Lansquenet, mon père. To fight for my people.
To save them from temptation.*
(Reynaud, p96)

Please read Using Connect Bible Studies *before leading a Bible study using this material.*

Opening Questions

Choose one of these questions.

Do you find chocolate irresistible? Why?	Empty a box of chocolates on a table. What is your reaction?
What is your favourite chocolate?	What chocolate would you choose as a gift and why?

Summary

Père Reynaud is parish priest in the provincial town of Lansquenet. His parishioners respect him and his call to abstinence for the time of Lent. Everything is nicely under control until Vianne Rocher arrives with her young daughter Anouk. Vianne does not struggle with temptation — for her, nothing is forbidden. With a flagrant disregard for the spiritual welfare of Reynaud's flock, she opens a chocolate shop right opposite the church. The shop and its exotic delights lure the parishioners in one by one. Frustrated, Reynaud establishes chocolate as the very essence of temptation — the ultimate indulgence during Lent. He himself takes pleasure in abstaining from more or less everything.

When Vianne announces her plans for an Easter Chocolate Festival, Reynaud's 'Bible groupies' get together to organise a campaign to stop her — the 'church versus chocolate' war is on. Ultimately, Reynaud's attempt to undermine Vianne fails — he only manages to set himself up for a fall. He launches a last minute attack on Vianne's festival, but even he cannot stand this final test. Alone in the shop early on Easter Sunday he stands amongst the chocolates holding a cudgel, intending to destroy her entire stock. The chocolates, however, get the better of him with their intoxicating presence, silently beckoning him to try one.

Before he knows it, Reynaud is gorging himself — in plain view of the square. The parishioners crowd round to see the unbelievable spectacle and Reynaud leaves in disgrace.

Key Issue: Temptation

Vianne provokes strong reactions when she opens her Chocolaterie in Lent in the middle of Lansquenet. She is both welcomed and shunned — because her exquisite wares represent temptation for many of the villagers. Temptation thus becomes a key theme of the book, as the various characters work out how to respond to chocolate. So is chocolate your biggest temptation? Would you too have found its taste and charms irresistible? Or are there other temptations which you struggle with? All of us face situations where we are tempted to do something, or think something, which we know we should not. What does the Bible say about the issues here? Where does temptation get its power? How do we deal with it, and what happens if we fail?

Bible Study

Choose one question from each section.

1. **The essence of temptation**

    The devil works not through evil but through weakness, père. You of all people know that. Without the strength and purity of our convictions, where are we? How secure are we? (Reynaud, p162)

    ♦ Read Genesis 3:1–13. Why was it wrong to eat the fruit? What was tempting about Satan's offer?

    ♦ Read Luke 4:1–13. What was the essence of the temptations Jesus faced? What was Jesus' perspective on the temptations?

2. **Temptations galore!**

    The creamy smell of chocolate is maddening. For a moment my senses are unnaturally enhanced; I can smell her perfume, a caress of lavender, the warm spicy scent of her skin ... Was this what you felt, mon père, that day in the old chancery? Did temptation wear this face? (Reynaud, p138)

    ♦ Read 1 Corinthians 10:1–13. What does this passage tell us about the universal nature of temptation? Read 1 Corinthians 6:12; 10:23–11:1. What does Paul say about the personal nature of some temptations? How does God help us with both the universal and personal temptations we face?

    Leaders: In 1 Corinthians 10:23–11:1, Paul is discussing the issue of food that has been sacrificed to idols. In pagan cultures, idolatry was so much part of life that much of the meat on sale in the markets would first have been offered to an idol. Clearly this was more concerning to some Christians than to others. See also 1 Corinthians 8.

- Read 1 John 2:15–17. In what ways are the temptations John writes about common to everybody? Read Romans 14:1–8. Is everyone tempted by the same things?

  Leaders: In Romans 14:1–4, Paul may not be referring specifically to food sacrificed to idols (see above), but to any moral restrictions that someone puts on their diet, which he says are a matter of conscience.

3. **Dealing with temptation**

   I have increased the austerity of my Lenten fast, choosing to continue even on the days when a relaxation is permitted ... I feel a prick of guilt at the thought that even my deprivation gives me pleasure, and I resolve to place myself in the path of temptation. I shall stand for five minutes at the window of the rôtisserie, watching the chickens on the spit. If Arnaud taunts me, so much the better. (Reynaud, p89)

   - Read Psalm 119:8–16; 33–40. How does the Psalmist deal with temptation? What is the balance between what the Psalmist does and what he asks God to do?

     See also Philippians 4:8, 9.

   - Read 1 Timothy 6:3–21. What are the keys to dealing with temptation?

4. **What happens when we've fallen?**

   It is like one of my dreams. I roll in chocolates. I imagine myself in a field of chocolates, on a beach of chocolates, basking-rooting-gorging ... The pig loses its cleverness in the face of so much delight, becomes a pig again, and though something at the top of my mind screams at me to stop I cannot help myself. Once begun it cannot end. This has nothing to do with hunger ...
   (Reynaud, p312)

   - Read 2 Samuel 12:1–25. How does God deal with David? How does David react to this? Does God's forgiveness mean that everything is resolved?

     See also Psalm 51.

   - Read 1 John 1:5–2:6. What does it mean to walk in the light when we have given in to temptation? What does this passage say about God's grace to people who have fallen?

     Leaders: Note that 'purifies' (v. 7) is in present continuous tense — ie 'the blood of Jesus, his Son, goes on purifying us from all sin.'

Implications

Chocolate, I am told, is not a moral issue. (Reynaud p209)

Choose one or more of the following questions.

- How could eating chocolate become a sin?

- How do we deal with issues which some people feel are wrong, but others are happy about?

- Is temptation worse if you are on your own? Can we help each other?

- What do we do with feelings we know are inappropriate or wrong?

- What would you say to a friend who sees the church as full of hypocrites like Curé Reynaud?

Prayer

Spend some time praying through these issues.

Background Reading

You will find links to some background reading on the Connect Bible Studies website: www.connectbiblestudies.com/uk/catalogue/0005/background.htm

Discuss

Discuss this study in the online discussion forums at www.connectbiblestudies.com/discuss

Members' Sheet: Chocolat — Part 1

Summary

Père Reynaud is parish priest in the provincial town of Lansquenet. His parishioners respect him and his call to abstinence for the time of Lent. Everything is nicely under control until Vianne Rocher arrives with her young daughter Anouk. Vianne does not struggle with temptation — for her, nothing is forbidden. With a flagrant disregard for the spiritual welfare of Reynaud's flock, she opens a chocolate shop right opposite the church. The shop and its exotic delights lure the parishioners in one by one. Frustrated, Reynaud establishes chocolate as the very essence of temptation — the ultimate indulgence during Lent. He himself takes pleasure in abstaining from more or less everything.

When Vianne announces her plans for an Easter Chocolate Festival, Reynaud's 'Bible groupies' get together to organise a campaign to stop her — the 'church versus chocolate' war is on. Ultimately, Reynaud's attempt to undermine Vianne fails — he only manages to set himself up for a fall. He launches a last minute attack on Vianne's festival, but even he cannot stand this final test. Alone in the shop early on Easter Sunday he stands amongst the chocolates holding a cudgel, intending to destroy her entire stock. The chocolates, however, get the better of him with their intoxicating presence, silently beckoning him to try one. Before he knows it, Reynaud is gorging himself — in plain view of the square. The parishioners crowd round to see the unbelievable spectacle and Reynaud leaves in disgrace.

Key Issue

Bible Study notes

Implications

Prayer

Discuss this with others on the Connect Bible Studies website: www.connectbiblestudies.com

Chocolat

Joanne Harris (Black Swan, 1999)

Part Two: Community

We have a new parishioner. A Vianne Rocher, a widow, I take it, with a young child ... she'll never fit in. A pleasant enough woman, but she has nothing in common with us. Give her two months, and she'll be back to the city where she belongs.
(Reynaud, p24)

Please read Using Connect Bible Studies *before leading a Bible study using this material.*

Opening Questions

Choose one of these questions.

Would you like to live in a small community like Lansquenet? Why?	Do you generally prefer large anonymous events or small gatherings? Why?
Would you rather live in a big city than where you are? Why?	Do you like people?

Summary

The sense of community in the small town of Lansquenet is very strong. For some, such as Caroline Clairmont, there is no question that every effort should be made to fit in — and keep undesirables out. Her behaviour towards newcomer Vianne, who has dared to open a chocolate shop during Lent, turns sour once she gets wind that Reynaud, the parish priest, disapproves. By contrast, Caroline's mother Armande delights in not being part of the community — she lives on her own down by the river out of everyone's way.

Armande and Vianne become friends on account of their shared differences. They welcome the invading community of river-gypsies who are despised by the likes of Caroline and Père Reynaud for their bohemian lifestyle. Unfortunately, Reynaud communicates his distaste for the gypsies to Paul-Marie Muscat who chooses to take matters into his own hands. A little petrol is all he needs to set light to and destroy the ringleader's boat. Devastated by the attack, the gypsies decide that they will have to move on — all except for ringleader Roux, who stays on in the hope of finding the arsonist. Accepted by Armande and Vianne, he finds work and eventually settles down. Vianne acknowledges her need to belong — perhaps Lansquenet will continue to be her home.

Key Issue: Community

We all live in community, whether we like it or not. Of course there are a few genuine hermits, but even they are reacting to something which is a given — we are born into relationship with other humans. So the vast majority of us experience community of one sort or other from our very first moments. *Chocolat* explores one particular type of small, enclosed community, which Vianne Rocher partly warms to and partly challenges. She does want to belong, but it is not easy. Some of us find we are members of many communities at once — for example, at work, in the home, in extended families or in social clubs. Was community God's idea in the first place? How can it best function? What are some dangers to avoid, and what does the Bible say about ideal community?

Bible Study

Choose one question from each section.

1. **The need for community**

    'Are we staying? Are we, Maman?' She tugs at my arm, insistently. 'I like it, I like it here. Are we staying?' ... Why not? It's as good a place as any. 'Yes, of course,' I tell her, my mouth in her hair. 'Of course we are.' Not quite a lie. This time it may even be true. (Vianne, p15)

    ♦ Read Ecclesiastes 4:7–12. What do we gain from being in community?

    ♦ Community is a theme that runs right through the Bible. We've chosen a few key passages — Genesis 1:26–27; 2:18–25; 11:1–9; Luke 6:32–36; Galatians 3:28; Revelation 7:9. What do these illustrate about God's view of community and its ultimate fulfilment?

2. **Community Expectations**

    'But the community ...' insisted Caroline. 'Surely you don't want people of that type — itinerants, thieves, Arabs for heaven's sake — ' ... 'It strikes me that the community should mind its own business,' I said tartly. 'It isn't up to me — or anybody — to decide how these people should live their lives.' (Vianne, p99)

    ♦ Read Luke 5:27–33. What kind of community did the Pharisees seem to want? How did Jesus' attitude conflict with the Pharisees' expectations?

    Leaders: Tax collectors were despised in Jesus' day. They were collaborators with the occupying Roman forces and were known for imposing higher taxes than the Romans required in order to grow rich themselves.

    ♦ Read Colossians 2:16–23. Why are these 'human commands' useless? What effect do they have on community life?

3. **Soured Community**

   Why can't they see what the woman is doing to us? Breaking down our community spirit, our sense of purpose. Playing on what is worst and weakest in the secret heart. Earning for herself a kind of affection, of loyalty which — God help me! — I am weak enough to covet. Preaching a travesty of goodwill, of tolerance, of pity for the poor homeless outcasts on the river while all the time the corruption grows deeper entrenched. (Reynaud, p162)

   - Read Jeremiah 23:9–22, 32. How were these prophets abusing their leadership? What impact did this have on their community?

   - Read Matthew 23:1–28. What were the leaders of Jesus' community doing wrong? Why was Jesus so angry about it?

4. **God's New Community**

   I could stay here, Maman. We have a home, friends. The weathervane outside my window turns, turns. Imagine hearing it every week, every year, every season. Imagine looking out of my window on a winter's morning. The new voice inside me laughs, and the sound is almost like coming home.
   (Vianne, p320)

   - Read Acts 2:42–47; 4:32–37. What was extraordinary about the early Christian community? Why was it like this?

   - Read Romans 12:1–21. What is the foundation for Christian community? How is this to be a model of good community?

Implications

If we are to stay we must be as like them as possible. (Vianne, p49)

Choose one or more of the following questions.

- How does your church compare to the early church community? What is your role within your church, and how can you help it to model good community?

- Have you fallen into the trap of placing expectations on others that are inappropriate for them? Or do you feel others do this to you?

- OK, so you think your church leaders/community leaders are not all they could be — what could you do that would help them?

- How can you be a positive and creative influence on your wider community?

- How would you talk about *Chocolat's* view of church community to a non-church-going friend?

Prayer

Pray for your church and community. Pray particularly for the leaders.

Background Reading

You will find links to some background reading on the Connect Bible Studies website: www.connectbiblestudies.com/uk/catalogue/0005/background.htm

Discuss

Discuss this study in the online discussion forums at www.connectbiblestudies.com/discuss

Members' Sheet: Chocolat — Part 2

Summary

The sense of community in the small town of Lansquenet is very strong. For some such as Caroline Clairmont, there is no question that every effort should be made to fit in — and keep undesirables out. Her behaviour towards newcomer Vianne, who has dared to open a chocolate shop during Lent, turns sour once she gets wind that Reynaud, the parish priest, disapproves. By contrast, Caroline's mother Armande delights in not being part of the community — she lives on her own down by the river out of everyone's way.

Armande and Vianne become friends on account of their shared differences. They welcome the invading community of river-gypsies who are despised by the likes of Caroline and Père Reynaud for their bohemian lifestyle. Unfortunately, Reynaud communicates his distaste for the gypsies to Paul-Marie Muscat who chooses to take matters into his own hands. A little petrol is all he needs to set light to and destroy the ringleader's boat. Devastated by the attack, the gypsies decide that they will have to move on — all except for ringleader Roux, who stays on in the hope of finding the arsonist. Accepted by Armande and Vianne, he finds work and eventually settles down. Vianne acknowledges her need to belong — perhaps Lansquenet will continue to be her home.

Key Issue

Bible Study notes

Implications

Prayer

Discuss this with others on the Connect Bible Studies website: www.connectbiblestudies.com

Chocolat

Joanne Harris (Black Swan, 1999)

Part Three: Friendship

'You have friends here,' I said gently. 'And even if you don't realize it yet, you're strong.'
(Vianne, p188)

Please read Using Connect Bible Studies *before leading a Bible study using this material.*

Opening Questions

Choose one of these questions.

Who is your best friend? Why?	What qualities do you look for in a friend?
When was the last time you made a new friend?	'There's only one thing better than a friend and that's a friend with chocolate.' Do you agree? Why?

Summary

Vianne Rocher arrives in the small French town of Lansquenet with the idea that this could be the start of a new era. Previously, she has never settled in one place long enough to make lasting friendships, but her young daughter, Anouk, is keen to try and begs her to let them stay. Vianne's new business is the perfect place to meet people and make friends — a chocolate shop, where customers are free to browse or sit down at the bar with a hot chocolate.

Everyone is welcome in Vianne's shop — even those who would rather she had not come to Lansquenet, such as the parish priest, Reynaud. He mistakes her warmth for a calculated attempt to lure his parishioners away from the church. In fact, she is merely offering the hand of friendship to those who often find themselves on the chilly fringes of the community through no fault of their own. The shop becomes a refuge for those who do not meet with the expectations of Lansquenet society — Joséphine — a battered wife; Armande — an elderly lady who refuses to give up life's pleasures for the sake of health; Roux — a homeless river-gypsy. It is through these friendships that Vianne finally knows what it means to belong.

Key Issue: Friendship

Vianne and Anouk want desperately to make friends in their new community. Vianne also wants to help the people she meets — she wants to be a good friend to them. Her involvement in their lives is pivotal for many of them, and important for her too. Without her attempts at friendship, there would be no plot for *Chocolat*. Similarly, many of us are deeply influenced by our friendships. Some of them are a joy, and some a heartache. Can the Bible help us to be a good friend to others? How do we know when to help our friends? Even more poignantly for many, how do we receive help when we are in need? How do we make and keep lasting friendships?

Bible Study

Choose one question from each section. One question in each of the four sections considers the friendship between David and Jonathan. You may like to use this as the basis for your entire study. If you do so, it would be good to read 1 Samuel 18:1–9; 20:1–42 as you begin.

1. Being a friend

Joséphine Muscat went by but did not stop ... I called to her, but she did not answer, quickening her step as if at some impending danger. I shrugged and let her go. These things take time. Sometimes for ever. (Vianne, p103)

- Focusing on 1 Samuel 18:1–9; 20:12–15, how did David and Jonathan express their friendship? Why might Jonathan's friendship with David be so unexpected?

- Read Romans 16. In what different ways were these people friends to Paul? How was Paul nurturing his friendships from a distance?

2. Giving help

If that stubbornness of hers could be turned out instead of in, what could she not achieve? I could do it, too. I could feel her thoughts, so close, welcoming me in. It would be so easy to take control ... I turned the thought aside impatiently. I had no right to force her to any decision. (Vianne, p111)

- Focusing on 1 Samuel 20:28–42, how did Jonathan help David? What motivated him?

- Read Matthew 25:31–46. What perspective on being a friend to others does Jesus give us?

3. **Receiving help**

   'We're still your friends,' I said as he reached the door. 'Armande and Luc and I. Don't be so defensive. We're trying to help you.' (Vianne, p212)

   ♦ Focusing on 1 Samuel 20:1–18, why does David flee to Jonathan? How does David express his dependence on Jonathan?

   ♦ Read Proverbs 11:25; 17:17; 18:24; 27:5–6, 9–10, 17. What do these verses tell us about receiving help from a friend?

4. **Keeping friends**

   'Joséphine, you're welcome to stay here for as long as you like. It's a pleasure to have you here.' (Vianne, p204)

   ♦ Focusing on 1 Samuel 20:14–17, 41, 42, how did David and Jonathan show the depth of their friendship? Why did they make such solemn vows?

   See also 1 Samuel 23:15–18; 2 Samuel 1:17–27 (note especially verse 26).

   ♦ Read 2 Timothy 1:1–7; 4:9–13. Why was Timothy's friendship precious to Paul? How does this compare to Paul's other friends? What does Paul want for Timothy?

   Leaders: 2 Timothy was Paul's final letter. When he wrote it, he was imprisoned in Rome and was facing imminent execution. This gives his words to Timothy an extra poignancy.

Implications

I understood that Armande Voizin does things in her own way, in her own time, refusing to be hurried or advised. I let her think it through. (Vianne, p84)

Choose one or more of the following questions.

- How pro-active are you about making friends?

- Some people seem to be friendly to everyone. What qualities in them make this possible and how could you develop them?

- Do you find it hard to receive help from others? If so, how might that affect them? How might it affect you?

- What are the best ways to help a friend in need — for example, recently bereaved/made redundant/homeless/pregnant/etc?

- Vianne used chocolate to put people at their ease and make friends. What are some alternatives?

Prayer

Spend some time praying through these issues.

Background Reading

You will find links to some background reading on the Connect Bible Studies website: www.connectbiblestudies.com/uk/catalogue/0005/background.htm

Discuss

Discuss this study in the online discussion forums at www.connectbiblestudies.com/discuss

Members' Sheet: Chocolat — Part 3

Summary

Vianne Rocher arrives in the small French town of Lansquenet with the idea that this could be the start of a new era. Previously, she has never settled in one place long enough to make lasting friendships, but her young daughter is keen to try and begs her to let them stay. Vianne's new business is the perfect place to meet people and make friends — a chocolate shop, where customers are free to browse or sit down at the bar with a hot chocolate.

Everyone is welcome in Vianne's shop — even those who would rather she had not come to Lansquenet, such as the parish priest, Reynaud. He mistakes her warmth for a calculated attempt to lure his parishioners away from the church. In fact, she is merely offering the hand of friendship to those who often find themselves on the chilly fringes of the community through no fault of their own. The shop becomes a refuge for those who do not meet with the expectations of Lansquenet society — Joséphine — a battered wife; Armande — an elderly lady who refuses to give up life's pleasures for the sake of health; Roux — a homeless river-gypsy. It is through these friendships that Vianne finally knows what it means to belong.

Key Issue

Bible Study notes

Implications

Prayer

Discuss this with others on the Connect Bible Studies website: www.connectbiblestudies.com

Chocolat

Joanne Harris (Black Swan, 1999)

Part Four: Change

But I could smell it too; the scent of the changing winds, the air of revelation. A distant scent of fire and ozone. A squeal of gears left long unused, the infernal machine of synchronicity.

(Vianne, p85)

Please read Using Connect Bible Studies *before leading a Bible study using this material.*

Opening Questions

Choose one of these questions.

Do you enjoy change?	Would you like to change the time of your Sunday services? Why/why not?
Do you long for the 'good old days'? Why/why not?	How many Christians does it take to change a light bulb?

Summary

The only constant thing in Vianne Rocher's life is change. As a child she was always on the move — her mother's desire to live in many places took them all over the world. However, when Vianne arrives in the small town of Lansquenet, it seems that her growing urge to settle down may at last be satisfied. Controversially, she opens a chocolate shop opposite the church just in time for Lent and soon has the measure of the townspeople's attitude to change as they tentatively visit her shop. As she gets to know them individually, she sees great potential for encouraging a few necessary changes. The person most in need of a change is Joséphine Muscat. Living in an abusive relationship has brought on all kinds of dysfunctional behaviour — including compulsive thieving. Vianne helps her to be strong enough to make the decision to leave her husband, whereupon she blossoms into a beautiful woman.

Père Reynaud, parish priest and driving force behind those who think Lansquenet should remain as it is, believes that Vianne is deliberately trying to undermine his authority and change the town for the worse. Vianne has no such agenda: 'I want to give, to make people happy; surely that can't do harm.' (p117)

Key Issue: Change

There is no escaping the fact that Vianne's arrival in Lansquenet brings lasting change. Her controversial actions challenge Lansquenet's traditional ways, and the sleepy little town changes for ever. Change is something we all have to face in our lives — growing up and growing old bring their own changes anyway, never mind the changes around us in our world. Sometimes we long to keep things the same, and sometimes we cannot wait for change. Whichever it is, change is here to stay. Does the Bible say anything to help us? How do we accept change? Are there times to resist it? What are the important changes that need welcoming into our lives?

Bible Study

Choose one question from each section.

1. **Transition — Facing Change**

    ... the wind, the carnival wind was still blowing, bringing with it the dim scent of grease and candyfloss and gunpowder, the hot sharp scents of the changing seasons, making the palms itch and the heart beat faster. For a time, then, we stay. For a time. Till the wind changes. (Vianne, p19)

    - Read Ecclesiastes 3:1–22. What does the writer of Ecclesiastes say we can expect from life 'under the sun'? How does 'eternity in the hearts of men' affect our perspective on change?

    - Read James 4:13–17. What attitude to life does James perceive in his readers? What does he say about our attitude to change? What other issues does he raise?

2. **Tradition — Resisting Change**

    In a place like Lansquenet, it sometimes happens that one person — schoolteacher, café proprietor, or priest — forms the lynchpin of the community. That this single individual is the essential core of the machinery which turns lives, like the central pin of a clock mechanism, sending wheels to turn wheels, hammers to strike, needles to point the hour. If the pin slips or is damaged, the clock stops. Lansquenet is like that clock, needles perpetually frozen at a minute to midnight, wheels and cogs turning uselessly behind the bland blank face. (Vianne, p43)

    - Read Acts 10:1–23. What change Peter was resisting? Why was the Lord's command so challenging?

    - Read Luke 9:57–62. What was the core issue for each of these three men? How did Jesus deal with them?

3. **Transfigure — Making Change**

   It's none of my business, of course. But I felt at that moment that if ever a place were in need of a little magic ... Old habits never die. And when you've once been in the business of granting wishes the impulse never quite leaves you. (Vianne, p19)

   - Read Judges 6:24–32. What was Gideon trying to change? How did his feelings affect the way he went about it?

     Leaders: Baal was the most significant of the Canaanite gods. Israel had never dealt decisively with pagan religion in the land. By this point in their history, the Israelites themselves had set up altars to Baal as well as Asherah poles. These were wooden representations of Asherah, a fertility goddess. Worship of both these deities often went together and was frequently lewd.

   - Read Acts 11:1–18. What change was Peter encouraging? Why was he so sure of himself?

4. **Transformation — Embracing Change**

   [Joséphine] is serene now, at peace with the world. I find myself becoming less and less so, in a perverse spirit of contradiction. And yet I envy her. It has taken so little to bring her to this state. A little warmth, a few borrowed clothes and the security of a spare room ... Like a flower she grows towards the light, without thinking or examining the process which moves her to do so. I wish I could do the same. (Vianne, p245)

   - Read James 1:19–25. What is the source of change in a believer's life? What is the process and target of change?

   - Read Colossians 3:1–17. Why does Paul say we must embrace change in our lives? What difference does this change make in our relationships?

Implications

Look at all the changes: me, Luc, Caro, the folks out on the river ... All of us changing. Speeding up. Like an old clock being wound up after years of telling the same time. (Armande, p124)

Choose one or more of the following questions.

- Why do we seek/resist change in our lives?

- Are there changes in your church/community you feel God wants you to make? How will you do it?

- Is there an area of your life that you need to change? Can your group help you with this?

- Who can you pray for today to make the greatest change of all — to acknowledge Jesus as Lord?

- How would you describe to a friend that Jesus brings greater potential for change than Vianne's chocolate?

Prayer

Spend some time praying through these issues.

Background Reading

You will find links to some background reading on the Connect Bible Studies website: www.connectbiblestudies.com/uk/catalogue/0005/background.htm

Discuss

Discuss this study in the online discussion forums at www.connectbiblestudies.com/discuss

Members' Sheet: Chocolat — Part 4

Summary

The only constant thing in Vianne Rocher's life is change. As a child she was always on the move — her mother's desire to live in many places took them all over the world. However, when Vianne arrives in the small town of Lansquenet, it seems that her growing urge to settle down may at last be satisfied. Controversially, she opens a chocolate shop opposite the church just in time for Lent and soon has the measure of the townspeople's attitude to change as they tentatively visit her shop. As she gets to know them individually, she sees great potential for encouraging a few necessary changes. The person most in need of a change is Joséphine Muscat. Living in an abusive relationship has brought on all kinds of dysfunctional behaviour — including compulsive thieving. Vianne helps her to be strong enough to make the decision to leave her husband, whereupon she blossoms into a beautiful woman.

Père Reynaud, parish priest and driving force behind those who think Lansquenet should remain as it is, believes that Vianne is deliberately trying to undermine his authority and change the town for the worse. Vianne has no such agenda: 'I want to give, to make people happy; surely that can't do harm.' (p117)

Key Issue

Bible Study notes

Implications

Prayer